THE
BETTER LETTER BOOK
A LETTER-WRITING GUIDE FOR KIDS • 3-6

WRITTEN BY DONNA GUTHRIE & JAN STILES
ILLUSTRATED BY BEV ARMSTRONG

The Learning Works

Copyright © 1994 – The Learning Works, Inc.

The Learning Works, Inc.

P.O. Box 6187
Santa Barbara, California 93160

STATE AND PROVINCE ABBREVIATIONS

UNITED STATES

Alabama	AL	Kentucky	KY	North Dakota	ND
Alaska	AK	Louisiana	LA	Ohio	OH
Arizona	AZ	Maine	ME	Oklahoma	OK
Arkansas	AR	Maryland	MD	Oregon	OR
California	CA	Massachusetts	MA	Pennsylvania	PA
Colorado	CO	Michigan	MI	Rhode Island	RI
Connecticut	CT	Minnesota	MN	South Carolina	SC
Delaware	DE	Mississippi	MS	South Dakota	SD
District of Columbia	DC	Missouri	MO	Tennessee	TN
Florida	FL	Montana	MT	Texas	TX
Georgia	GA	Nebraska	NE	Utah	UT
Hawaii	HI	Nevada	NV	Vermont	VT
Idaho	ID	New Hampshire	NH	Washington	WA
Illinois	IL	New Jersey	NJ	West Virginia	WV
Indiana	IN	New Mexico	NM	Wisconsin	WI
Iowa	IA	New York	NY	Wyoming	WY
Kansas	KS	North Carolina	NC		
Puerto Rico	PR	Virgin Islands	VI	American Samoa	AS
Guam	GU				

CANADA

Alberta	AL	Newfoundland	NF	Prince Edward Island	PE
British Columbia	BC	Northwest Territories	NT	Quebec	PQ
Manitoba	MB	Nova Scotia	NS	Saskatchewan	SK
New Brunswick	NB	Ontario	ON	Yukon Territory	UT

CONTENTS

The Better Letter Book
© The Learning Works, Inc.

To the Teacher or Parent

Writing letters can be fun for kids. There are many easy ways to bring letter writing into the daily lives of children. *The Better Letter Book* provides activities to help young writers ages eight through twelve master the art of correspondence. Children learn about the parts of a letter, the different types of letters, and ways to make their letters creative, interesting, and effective. Exercises in this book can also be used as supplemental language activities for children who are learning English. Because letter writing is a shorter version of storytelling, letters can be a nice bridge to longer, more descriptive writing.

The Better Letter Book is divided into four parts. The first section, **Learning About Letters**, introduces the two basic kinds of letters. Exercises help students become familiar with the parts of a letter and how to use them.

The second and third sections provide a variety of letter-writing skills. The second section, **Friendly Letters**, helps young writers make their letters to friends or relatives more personal, interesting, and entertaining. It provides guidelines for thank-you letters, invitations, letters of congratulations, letters of sympathy or condolence, and apologies. Part three, **Action Letters**, introduces techniques for writing business letters. It covers complaints, complimentary letters, "op-ed" letters, requests for information, and letters to support a cause.

In these middle sections, the workbook identifies three basic components or types of information that should be included in the body of each kind of letter. By looking for the numbers **1**, **2**, and **3**, young writers can see exactly what they need to include to make their letters clear and effective.

The final section, **In the Mailbag**, provides information on addresses, postal codes, and stamps. It explains how to make postcards and decorate stationery.

Most activities are explained on a left-hand page, with an accompanying activity on the right-hand page. After taking your young writer through the introductory material appropriate to his or her knowledge and skill level, you can use the activities in varied order. While some pages work best as a group (such as the activities for writing to a friend or the pages on "Writing for a Cause" and "Writing to Public Officials"), most activities can be used individually as a need for the skill arises. Throughout the book, **Mailbox Messages** give reminders, tips, and additional information.

All About Letters

The U.S. Post Office handles 110 billion pieces of mail a year. That's enough mail to fill 440,000 railroad cars. If you lined up all those cars, they'd stretch from New York City to Disneyland. In all that mail, there might be a letter for you.

How does it feel to open the mailbox and find a letter just for you? You can make your friends and relatives feel special just by writing and sending them letters.

Have you written letters before? How many? Only one? A few? A whole bunch? Write your answer here.

_____

Think about why you wrote some of these letters. For fun? To say thank you? To right a wrong? Write some of the reasons here.

_____

_____

_____

_____

Think of a friend or relative who would like to get a letter from you. Write the person's name here.

_____

Two Kinds of Letters

Every letter you write will be either a friendly letter or a business letter.

You write **friendly letters** to friends, relatives, or acquaintances — to people you already know.

Friendly letters are like conversations on paper. You express your thoughts or feelings, share your news, extend an invitation, or say thank you.

You write **business letters** to companies, organizations, and elected or public officials — to people you **don't** know personally.

Business letters are action letters. Anybody can write them. In business or action letters, you express an opinion or concern, make a complaint, request information, or ask someone to take action.

Your Turn: Pick the Letter

For each of the letters below, decide whether you would write a friendly letter or a business letter.

Write an **F** in the blank if you would write a friendly letter. Write a **B** if you would write a business letter.

_____ to thank your favorite uncle for a gift

_____ to ask a store owner to sponsor a school festival

_____ to tell the mayor a broken stoplight needs fixing

_____ to invite your cousin to visit you this summer

_____ to ask a legislator to support protection for wildlife

_____ to express sympathy for a friend whose pet has died

_____ to apologize to a friend for losing your temper and hurting the person's feelings

_____ to tell a company president to change a TV ad because the toy doesn't do what the ad showed

_____ to thank your coach for helping you improve your batting

_____ to write the newspaper editor about why it's important to pass a no-smoking law

Parts of a Letter

Letters can have as many as seven parts. Let's learn about these parts.

- **The heading** includes your name and address. If you have your own stationery, it may already have your name and address printed. That's called letterhead stationery.

- **The date** should be the month, date, and year you write the letter.

- **The inside address** includes the name and address of the person to whom you are writing. Sometimes it includes the person's title and a company name.

- **The greeting** is also called the **salutation**. It usually begins with "Dear."

- **The body** of the letter is what you want to say. Look for the numbers **1**, **2**, and **3** in this book. They will show you what to put in the body of each kind of letter.

- **The closing** comes right before you sign your name. The most common closing is "Sincerely."

- **The signature** is where you sign your name.

Your Turn: Label the Parts

Can you label the parts in this letter? Write the name of each part on one of the lines. Then draw an arrow to the correct example in the letter.

MAILBOX TIP
The parts of this letter are in the same order as the list on page 8.

Donna Guthrie and Jan Stiles
123 Author Road
Letterhead, California 95070

March 17, 1994

Ms. Rita Book, President
ABC Publishing Co.
P.O. Box 0000
Bookville, California 90000

Dear Ms. Book:

Everyone needs to know how to write letters. We write letters to get a job, to say thank you, to extend sympathy, and just to keep in touch with friends.

Many children think letter writing is too hard. It's not. Children write great letters when they try. With a little help, everyone can learn to write good letters.

We'd like to offer some help in a workbook that shows children how letter writing can be as easy as 1-2-3. Would you like to see a sample of our book?

Sincerely,

Donna Guthrie   Jan Stiles

Donna Guthrie and Jan Stiles

_____

_____

_____

_____

_____

_____

_____

Which Parts Mean Business?

Business or action letters need all seven parts of a letter. Because you want action or a reply, you need to include a heading with your name and address.

Always put an inside address after the date. Remember to include the name of the person to whom you're writing, his or her title if you know it, the company or organization name if there is one, and the address.

In a business letter, always put a colon after the name in the salutation.

Print or type your name under your signature. If you're writing as an officer for a club, your school, or an organization, add your title.

> **MAILBOX TIP**
> If you don't know the name of the person to whom you need to write, use a title in the salutation. Write "Dear Superintendent" or "Dear Editor."
> If you do know the person's name, use "Mr." for a man and "Ms." for a woman.

Closing a Business Letter

The closing in a business letter is usually more formal than in a friendly letter. For example, it is customary to show respect for an elected or public official by closing with "Respectfully yours." Here are some good closings for business letters:

Sincerely,
Sincerely yours,
Respectfully yours,
Truly yours,

1. How many parts are there in a business or action letter? _____

2. How would you close a letter to the president of the United States or the prime

   minister of Canada? _____

Which Parts Are Friendly?

Friendly letters need only five parts. When you write to people you know, you don't have to include a heading with your name and address. You don't need an inside address.

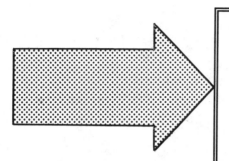

MAILBOX REMINDER

PARTS OF A FRIENDLY LETTER

Date
Greeting
Body or Message
Closing
Your Signature

Closings for Friendly Letters

You can use almost anything to close a friendly letter. Here are some friendly closings:

Love,
With love,
Your friend,
Sincerely,
Thank you,
Best wishes,
See you soon,
Miss you,

SEE YOU LATER!

Make up your own closing for each letter listed here.

to your brother, sister, or cousin _____

to your best friend _____

to your pet or a friend's pet _____

to your funniest or craziest relative _____

Six Steps to Great Letters

Here are six steps to help you write great letters. Keep this list handy so you can use it when you need help.

- **Plan**

  Plan your letter. Why are you writing? What kind of letter will you write? Do you know the correct address? Do you have the information you need? What stationery is best — large or small paper, note paper, a postcard, or something else?

- **List**

  List the main topics you want to write about. Put the most important one first. Add details or examples. Decide the best order.

- **Draft**

  Use pencil and write a "rough draft." Don't worry about spelling and punctuation. Just get your ideas on paper. For a long letter to a close friend, making notes may be enough. For a letter to a company or public official, draft the whole letter.

- **Proofread**

  Read your draft. Better yet, read it out loud. How does it sound? Did you leave anything out? Correct the spelling, punctuation, and grammar. You may want to ask someone to read your draft to be sure it's clear.

- **Write**

  Copy your draft neatly in pen (or use a typewriter or computer). Read your letter one last time. Correct any mistakes.

- **Address**

  Address your envelope accurately and neatly. Use the correct postage. Remember that sending letters to other countries will require more postage.

Writing Friendly Letters

Friendly letters are the easiest to write — and the most fun. They are a good way to keep in touch with friends or relatives you don't see every day. You can also write friendly letters to people you work with, like your teachers or club leaders.

Sometimes you need to write a particular kind of friendly letter. In these letters, you follow certain rules about what to write and how to say it.

You can write friendly letters to . . .

- thank someone for a gift or a favor
- thank someone for having you visit
- congratulate a friend
- invite someone for a visit or a special occasion
- offer your sympathy for a friend's loss
- send a get-well message to someone who's sick or hurt
- apologize for hurting someone's feelings or making a mistake

What friendly letters have you had to write?

Look at the list on this page. Have you had to write any of these kinds of letters? List them here.

_____

_____

_____

_____

_____

The Better Letter Book
© The Learning Works, Inc.

Good-Looking Friendly Letters

Friendly letters that look good are easier and more enjoyable to read. Use your best handwriting. If your stationery has lines, stay on them.

Leave space (called margins) on both sides and at the top and bottom of your stationery. Don't write to the edge of the page. If your paper has pictures or a design, write around the design (unless it's very faint and covers most of the page).

Here are some other guidelines:

- Write the date at the top, usually on the right side of the paper. Leave space between the date and the greeting, and between the greeting and the body.

- Indent the first line of each paragraph.

- Leave space between the body of your letter and the closing. Sign your name directly under the closing.

Here is a good-looking friendly letter. Use it as a model.

August 18, 1995

Dear Erin,

I rode my bike past your old house today and thought of you. It's been three weeks since you moved, but it seems a lot longer.

School starts in a couple of weeks. It's weird to think about being in sixth grade without you. Does it feel weird to you, too?

Only two good things have happened since you moved. First, Rosy had her puppies. She had two males, both brown with black, just like her, and one honey-colored female which is the cutest of all.

The other good thing is that the poem I wrote about our crazy picnic was published in the school magazine. I'm sending you a copy.

So how do you like it there? Have you met any new friends or gone to visit your new school? Send me a picture of your house. Having a park across the street sounds neat.

Did you find a new gymnastics coach? Don't give it up. You're too good to quit. Besides, I always wanted to have a friend in the Olympics, and you're my best chance.

I miss you a lot. Nobody makes me laugh like you do.

Love,
Tony

Name _____

Your Turn:
Greetings and Closings

Think of three friends and two relatives to whom you could write friendly letters.

On the lines below, write the greeting. The most common is "Dear," followed by the person's name and a comma. Then write the closing you would use for each person.

Friend Number 1

greeting _____ closing _____

Friend Number 2

greeting _____ closing _____

Friend Number 3

greeting _____ closing _____

Relative Number 1

greeting _____ closing _____

Relative Number 2

greeting _____ closing _____

Making a List

Letters to your friends should be tailor-made. What you write should suit one person and no one else.

Before you begin writing, think about what makes this person special. Make a short list of things you want to tell this particular friend. Think of things you have in common.

What You Can Write

You can write about what's happening in your life. Tell your friend about . . .

- your family or pets
- your school
- your activities or clubs

You might write about things you have in common, like . . .

- a hobby you both enjoy
- a sport you both play
- a place you went together

You might share how you feel about . . .

- a change in your life
- an idea you want to try
- a problem you have

ASK QUESTIONS!

Don't just write about yourself. Ask what your friend is thinking, planning, and doing.

Good letters are like conversations. You don't do all the talking.

Your Turn: Make a List

Think of a friend or relative who would enjoy getting a letter from you. After you write your letter, mail it or deliver it in person.

On the next few pages, you'll plan a letter to write to your friend or relative.

Make a list of things you can write to your friend.

The friend I will write to is _____

List three things you will tell your friend.

1. _____

_____

2. _____

_____

3. _____

_____

Write two questions you will ask your friend.

1. _____

_____

2. _____

_____

The Better Letter Book
© The Learning Works, Inc.

Things to Enclose

Letters give you a chance to share things with friends. Here are some ideas for things you can send with your letters.

- Cut out comics, cartoons, or jokes to send.

- Include poems or riddles you wrote or ones you cut from magazines.

- Clip and send newspaper stories about people or places you and your friend both know.

- Enclose addresses for contests, special offers, or free gifts.

- Send the scores or results from your latest games or competitions.

- Copy recipes for foods you and your friend both like or for dishes you can use on a special occasion, like a camping trip or a picnic.

Think of the friend you named on page 17. Describe two things you can enclose with your letter. Use the list above for ideas or think of your own.

The friend I'm writing to is _____

Two things I can enclose are:

1. _____

2. _____

Things to Do

Letters to friends should be fun to write and fun to read. Here are some ideas to make your letters more fun.

- Make up a code. You might replace each letter with a number, symbol, or other letter. Use the code and send your friend a copy.
- Spell words backwards. Write the whole letter this way or just certain words.
- Try mirror writing. Look at your paper in a mirror. Print so the words can be read only in the mirror. Pick one word or try several. This takes practice, so be patient.

- Write with your pen in your other hand, your foot, or your teeth. Tell your friend how you wrote your letter.
- Add your own drawings, maps, or illustrations.
- Cut letters, words, or pictures from magazines. Paste them in your letter.
- Use different colored pens or pencils.

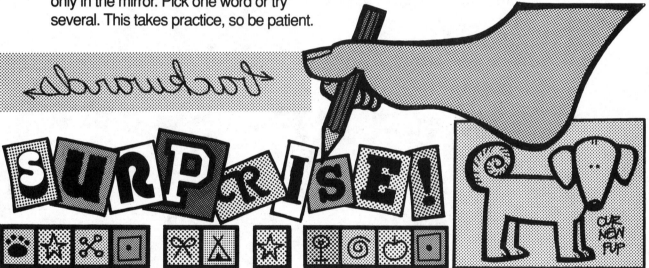

Think of the friend you named on page 17. Describe one thing you can do to make a letter to that friend more fun. Use the list above for ideas or make up your own.

The friend I'm writing to is _____

What I will do to make a letter to my friend more fun is: _____

_____

_____

_____

Stories to Tell

When you write to a friend about something that happened, tell it like a story. Give your story a beginning, a middle, and an end. Make it exciting, funny, or mysterious. Use descriptive words. End with a surprise or a punch line, which is the last and funniest line of a joke.

What story could you write to a friend? Here are a few ideas:

- an adventure you had with your pet
- something going on in your town or school
- something you tried that went wrong
- a funny thing that happened when something broke

Write a story for a letter to the friend you named before. If you want, choose from your list on page 17.

I am writing this story for a letter to _____

Your Turn: Write Your Letter

Write a letter to the friend you named before. Decide what stationery you will use. Be sure to include all the parts of a friendly letter. When you're done, mail or deliver your letter.

If you need help addressing the envelope, look at page 59.

If you want to make your own stationery, see page 63.

MAILBOX REMINDER

PARTS OF A FRIENDLY LETTER
Date
Greeting
Body or Message
Closing
Your Signature

In your letter, try to include:

- the three things and two questions you listed on page 17
- the things you planned to enclose (see page 18)
- something you planned to do to make your letter more fun (see page 19)
- the story you wrote on page 20

Terrific Thank-You's for Gifts

Writing terrific thank-you notes for gifts is as easy as 1-2-3. You don't have to write a lot, but you should include these three things:

❶ A thank-you for the gift

❷ Something specific about the gift, such as how you will use it, how it will help you, or how much you like it

❸ A second thank-you, often using the word "again"

> **MAILBOX REMINDER**
> - **Use the seven-day rule. Write within one week.**
> - **Mention the gift and say something specific about it.**

Here's an example:

April 12, 1996

Dear Uncle Matthew,

    Thank you for the flashlight you gave me for my birthday.

    It will be perfect for camping this summer, especially since I dropped my old one in the lake last year.

    Thank you again for lighting up my birthday.

            Love,
            Billy

Date

Greeting

❶ Thank you

❷ Something specific about the gift

❸ Second thank you

Closing

Signature

Your Turn: Something Specific

Think of two gifts you have received in the past. Write the gift and its giver below. Then write something specific about each gift.

gift _____ giver _____

something specific_____

_____

_____

gift _____ giver _____

something specific_____

_____

_____

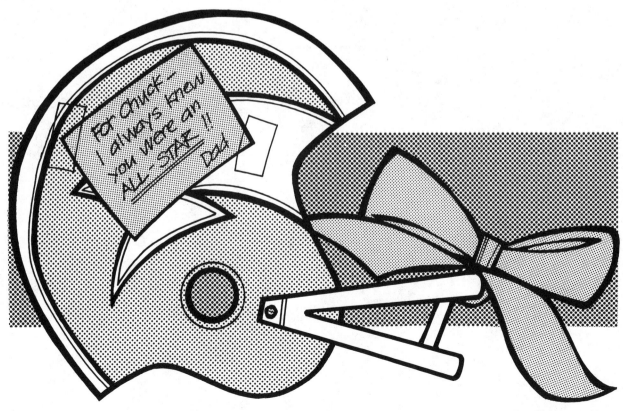

Thank You for the Favor

Someone who does you a favor has taken the time to help you or to do something nice. Saying thank you makes both you and the person who helped you feel good.

You write a thank-you note for a favor the same way you write one for a gift. Instead of saying thank you for what someone gave you, you express your appreciation for what someone did.

Use the same 1-2-3's you would use to thank someone for a gift.

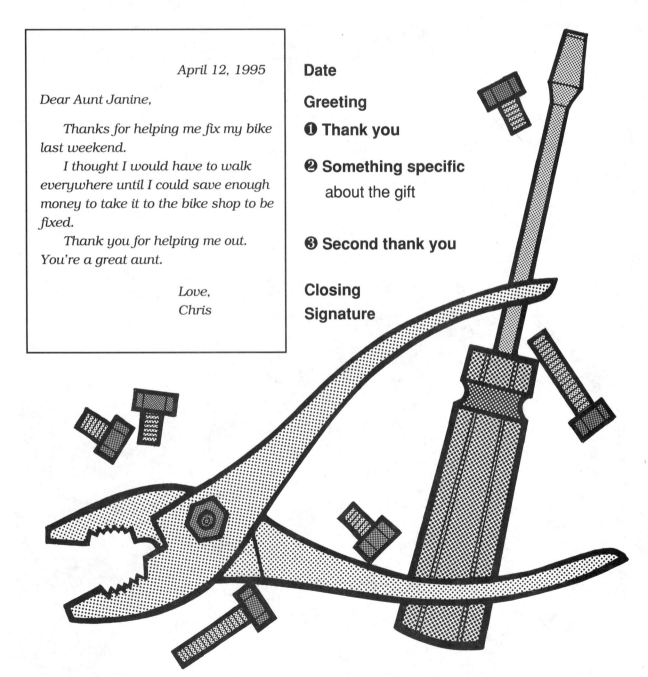

April 12, 1995

Dear Aunt Janine,

    Thanks for helping me fix my bike last weekend.
    I thought I would have to walk everywhere until I could save enough money to take it to the bike shop to be fixed.
    Thank you for helping me out. You're a great aunt.

        Love,
        Chris

Date

Greeting

❶ **Thank you**

❷ **Something specific**
   about the gift

❸ **Second thank you**

Closing

Signature

Name _____

Your Turn: Say Thank You

Think of someone who gave you a gift or did you a favor. Write a short note to say thank you. Remember your 1-2-3's.

The person I am writing to is _____

Thank You for the Hospitality

When someone invites you to a party or for a visit, the friendly thing to do is write a thank-you note as soon as you return home. These thank-you's are often called bread-and-butter notes. Why do you think they got that name?

When you write, remember to include the 1-2-3's for thank-you notes.

> **MAILBOX REMINDER**
> - Remember the seven-day rule. Write within one week of your visit.
> - Always say thank you, whether or not you had a great time.

Here is an example.

Sept. 2, 1994

Dear Grandma and Grandpa,

    Thank you for having me visit the farm this summer.

    I loved riding the horse. I even liked doing chores with Grandpa. The fair was great fun, too.

    Thank you again for letting me visit. It was a great summer.

              Lots of love,
              Mandy

❶ **Thank you**

❷ **Something specific** about your visit

❸ **Second thank you**

Your Turn: A Costume Party

Practice saying thanks for a friend's hospitality. Fill in the blanks below.

Imagine a friend invited you to a costume party. You went dressed as a

_____ and won second prize for best costume. Your friend

wore a _____ costume. Your friend's mother baked some

delicious _____ for the party.

Now write the 1-2-3's for the body of a short letter thanking your friend for the party.

❶ _____

_____

❷ _____

_____

_____

_____

❸ _____

_____

_____

Inviting Friends to Share the Fun

Friends can make a birthday, a movie, or a baseball game even more fun.

If you're inviting just one or two friends, it's easier to call to make the arrangements. If you're having a group of friends, a letter of invitation is the best way to make sure all your guests get the information they need.

The 1-2-3's of Inviting a Group

❶ **The invitation:** Tell what kind of event or party you're having.

❷ **The details:** Give the date, time, place, and all other information.

❸ **Request for response:** Tell the person you're inviting when and how to contact you.

R.S.V.P.

R.S.V.P. stands for the French phrase *Répondez s'il vous plaît*. It means "Please respond."

Put R.S.V.P. on your invitation with your phone number so people can tell you if they are coming.

November 4, 1996

Dear Gretchen,

I'm inviting a few friends to an ice skating party for my birthday. I'd like you to come.

We'll meet at the Ice Palace rink in Snow Valley Mall on Winter Road. Be at the entrance at 2:00 p.m. on Saturday, November 14.

We'll rent skates there, or you can bring your own. My dad will pay for the skates if you rent them. Afterwards we'll have pizza, drinks, and cake and ice cream. My dad will drive you home.

Call me by Wednesday to let me know if you can come. Dad has to make the reservations.

Hope you can come,
Sally

R.S.V.P. 555-1730

Date

Greeting

❶ **Invitation**

❷ **Details**

❸ **Request for response**

Closing
Signature

R.S.V.P.

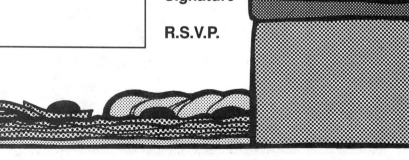

Your Turn: Invite a Group

Write a letter you could send to five friends, inviting them to a sleep-over party. Have everyone bring a favorite video game. Remind your friends to bring pajamas and whatever they need to spend the night. Remember to follow the numbers, 1-2-3.

Do you need to include any special information or instructions about what video games people can bring? Remember to include an R.S.V.P. in your invitation.

The Better Letter Book
© The Learning Works, Inc.

Let's Get Together

Inviting a friend to stay overnight is usually done with a phone call. But if your friend lives far away and is visiting for more than a day, it's best to put everything in a letter.

A letter lets you be a good host right from the start. Your friend can use your letter as a checklist for packing and can refer to it for details about clothes, money, and plans.

The 1-2-3's of Inviting a Friend

❶ **The invitation**

❷ **The details:** Begin with dates and times for the visit. Add any other information, like travel arrangements, special plans, and what to bring.

❸ **Request for response:** Include instructions for how your friend should contact you or when you will call to confirm the visit.

> **REMEMBER**
> Even when you write a letter, it's best to have your mom or dad phone to confirm all the details.

May 15, 1997

Dear Nathan,

My family is going camping this summer, and Mom and Dad said I can bring a friend. I'd like you to come.

We'll be camping at Lake Powell from August 6 to August 13. Dad wants to get on the road early, so you will need to sleep here August 5.

We're taking our boat, so bring a towel and your swimsuit. We have life jackets and fishing poles, but you'll need a sleeping bag. And don't forget hiking shoes and money for souvenirs.

Write as soon as you can to tell me if you can come.

Your camping buddy,
Sam, the Fishin' Man

❶ **Invitation**

❷ **Details**

❸ **Request for response**

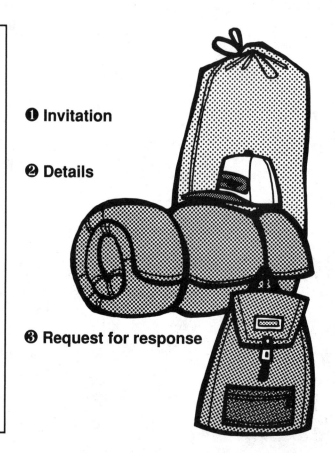

Your Turn: Invite a Friend

Practice your invitation skills by writing a letter to a friend or cousin in another city. Ask your friend or cousin to come with you on your week-long family vacation.

Decide where you will go. Just be sure to give all the information your friend or cousin will need to have a wonderful trip.

If you need help, look at the example on page 30.

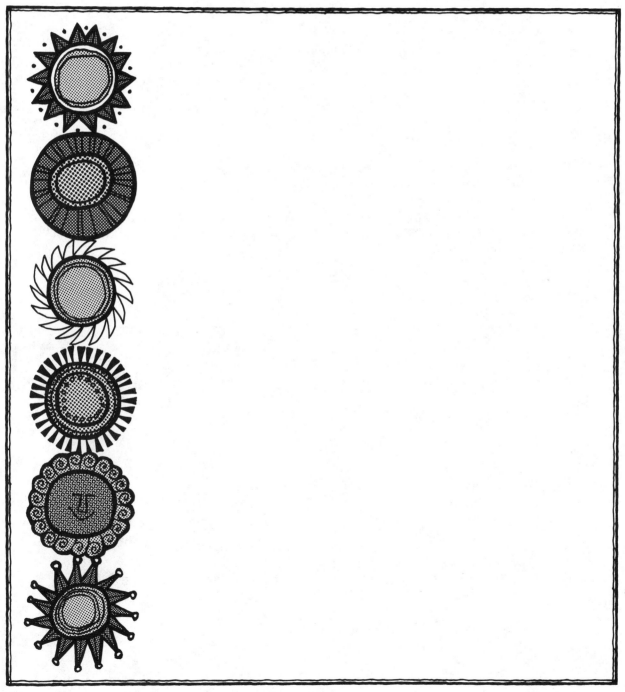

How to Write an Apology

Everyone makes mistakes. Everybody has broken something, told a secret, said something unkind, or been mean to someone. When you hurt a friend's feelings, the best thing to do is apologize.

An apology puts the problem behind you. You don't have to keep worrying about your mistake. A written apology shows you are serious and sincere about making things better. It's often easier to admit you were wrong in a letter than to say it face-to-face.

```
MAILBOX TIP
■ Keep your letter short.
■ Admit what you did — no excuses.
■ Say how you feel. Be honest.
```

The 1-2-3's of Writing an Apology

❶ **Apologize:** Say you are sorry and tell what you're sorry for. Explain your actions if you can, but don't make excuses. Admit your mistake.

❷ **Make amends:** Tell how you plan to make up for your mistake. If you need to pay for something you've broken or replace something you've lost, tell what you will do and when you will do it.

❸ **Ask forgiveness:** Repeat your apology and ask to be forgiven. Say what you hope the result of your letter will be.

August 6, 1995

Dear Colin,

I'm sorry that when I borrowed your new bike, it was stolen. I left it outside the arcade for just a minute, and I didn't think I needed to lock it for this quick stop.

My father said he'll replace your bike, and I'll work Saturdays at his store to pay him back.

I shouldn't have left your bike unlocked. I hope you will accept my apology and forgive me. You're a good friend, and I don't want to lose your friendship.

Sincerely,

Brian

❶ **Apologize**

❷ **Make amends**

❸ **Ask forgiveness**

Your Turn: Say You're Sorry

Read this story about what happened to Trevor. Then, pretend you are Trevor and write a letter to admit what you did and to say you're sorry.

When Marco's father lost his job, Marco was worried and upset. He needed someone to talk to, so he told his best friend Trevor what had happened. "But my mom and dad told me not to tell anybody," Marco said. "So promise you won't tell, OK?"

Trevor promised. But the next day in the lunchroom, Amanda asked why Marco wasn't playing with his friends anymore. Trevor told Amanda what had happened to Marco's dad. "I'm only telling because I know you can keep a secret. Marco wasn't supposed to tell anyone."

Unfortunately, someone at a nearby table overheard. Now the news is all over school. Marco is hurt, embarrassed, and angry.

The Better Letter Book
© The Learning Works, Inc.

Letters to Congratulate

It's fun to celebrate good things that happen to your friends and family. Everyone enjoys having an honor or accomplishment recognized. When you write letters to congratulate people for their achievements, you share in their pride and happiness.

The 1-2-3's of Saying "Congratulations!"

❶ **Congratulations:** Congratulate the person on what happened and tell how and where you heard about it.

❷ **Something specific:** Say something specific about the good news, like how much it's deserved, how hard the person worked, or what might happen next.

❸ **Second congratulations:** Repeat your congratulations and say how happy you are for the person.

> **MAILBOX TIP**
> When you see good news about a friend in the newspaper, cut out the picture and/or story to send with a note of congratulations.
>   Write the name and date of the paper in the margin of the article.

Who deserves a letter of congratulations?

- a friend who graduates
- your cousin who gets engaged to be married
- your grandparents on their anniversary
- your aunt who has a new baby
- a neighbor who achieves a major goal, like climbing a mountain or getting a job or promotion
- a friend who receives an award or honor, wins a contest, gets a scholarship, or is elected to office

Who else can you think of? Write some examples of your own.

_____

_____

_____

Your Turn: Praise for Pat

Imagine you found this news story about your friend Pat in the local newspaper. Write a letter of congratulations to Pat.

Student Honored for Science

Pat Wu, a student in the sixth grade at Parkmore School, won the grand prize for best overall project at the county science fair. Wu demonstrated energy sources that are pollution-free and that don't rely on limited natural resources.

The young scientist has entered the fair for the past four years and has won first prize in the upper elementary division for two of those years. This is the sixth grader's first grand prize. Winning it qualifies Wu to compete in the state fair to be held in Springfield in March.

CONGRATULATIONS!

The Better Letter Book
© The Learning Works, Inc.

How to Show a Friend You Care

When someone dies, it's hard to know what to say. Most people feel awkward and uncomfortable. Those feelings are normal.

One way you can show you care is to write a sympathy or condolence letter. These letters are probably the most difficult to write, but they can also be the most appreciated.

Try to think how you would feel if you lost someone important to you. When you're sad, it helps to know that people care. In your letter, assure the person that you do care. Try to mention happier times or a special memory of the person who has passed away.

> **MAILBOX TIP**
> Write your sympathy letters by hand, not on a computer or typewriter.

The 1-2-3's of Sympathy Letters

❶ **Condolence:** Say how sad your were to learn of the death. You might mention how you found out.

❷ **Something specific:** Tell why you'll miss the person or why you thought he or she was special. Describe a happy memory you have of that person.

❸ **Second condolence:** Express your sorrow again and offer your help.

Here's an example of a sympathy letter.

> *July 16, 1995*
>
> *Dear Gina,*
>
> *I was so sorry to hear that your grandmother died. I know how special she was to you.*
>
> *Remember when I met her at your house? Her stories really made me laugh. Nobody knew as much about baseball as she did.*
>
> *I just want you to know how sorry I am. You're lucky to have had a grandmother like her and to have so many wonderful memories.*
>
> *In sincere sympathy,*
> *Ralph Hon*

❶ **Condolence**

❷ **Something specific**

❸ **Second condolence**

Your Turn: Show You Care

Now practice writing a sympathy letter. Think of a friend or a famous person who has had a death in the family. If you can't think of an actual person to write to, make someone up.

How to Show Others You Care

Sometimes you know the person who has died but not the family member who is grieving. Then you'll need to write your letter of condolence like this.

❶ **Introduction:** Tell who you are and explain how you knew the person who died.

❷ **Something specific:** Describe something you remember about the person or explain why you wanted to write.

❸ **Condolence:** Express your sorrow.

Here's how:

> *April 20, 1996*
>
> *Dear Mrs. Santos,*
>
> *I was on the same soccer team as Miguel, and I also knew him at school. I just heard that he died in a car accident.*
>
> *Miguel was a great soccer player and one of the nicest guys on the team. He taught me to do kicks on goal and always laughed at my dumb jokes. I wanted to tell you how special he was to me.*
>
> *I'm so sorry about what happened. I know you'll miss Miguel more than anything. I will miss him, too.*
>
> *My deepest sympathy,*
> *Jeff Kelly*

❶ **Introduction**

❷ **Something specific**

❸ **Condolence**

Your Turn: Lincoln's Wife

If you are writing a sympathy letter to someone you don't know, here are a few phrases to help you.

- I offer my deepest sympathy.
- I was so sorry to hear about your loss.
- I hope your memories will comfort you.
- Please let me know how I can help.
- If there's anything I can do, please call.

> **Sympathy letters keep giving comfort because they can be read again and again.**

Now write to Mrs. Lincoln about the death of her husband, Abraham.

Your Turn: Sharing Sympathy

Sympathy letters can be written for other reasons, too. You can share your sympathy with a friend who . . .

- lost a pet that ran away
- lost something because of a fire, an accident, or a natural disaster
- was injured in an accident
- is sick and in the hospital

> **MAILBOX TIP:**
> GET-WELL LETTERS
>
> Letters to friends who are injured or sick are called get-well letters. Here's what to write:
> ❶ Condolence
> ❷ Something specific
> ❸ Get-well wish — "*I hope you're better soon and back playing baseball.*"

Pick one of the people below and write a short sympathy letter. Make up whatever you'd like about the person you choose.

- Write to Carol, whose cat ran away.
- Write to Jim, who lost his house in a fire.
- Write to your teacher, Mr. Farentino, who failed to make the Olympic wrestling team after years of practice.
- Write to Kate, who broke her arm while competing in a skateboarding contest.

Your Turn: Pick a Letter

Now that you've learned about different kinds of friendly letters, practice writing your own. Choose one of the special letters listed below. Make up an imaginary friend to write to, or use a real one.

Thank-you letter
- for a gift
- for a favor
- for hospitality

Letter of invitation
- to invite a group of friends
- to invite one friend for a long visit

Sympathy or condolence letter
- to a friend who has had a family member die
- to the parent of a friend who has died
- to a friend who is injured or ill, has lost something important, or has had a disappointment

Write your letter here.

The Better Letter Book
© The Learning Works, Inc.

Writing Action Letters

You don't have to be in business to write a business letter!

Have you ever ordered something in the mail, returned a product, or ordered a part? Have you ever wanted to request a free sample or to complain about an unfair situation?

To do any of these things, you would write a business or action letter. You can write to companies, politicians, and newspaper or magazine editors. All you need is a goal or purpose — something you want to do or get done. Business letters ask for action.

Here is a model you can use when you write business letters.

> Grayson Parks
> 1020 Abracadabra Road
> Houdini, Ohio 43012
>
>
> April 28, 1996
>
>
> Illusions Plus
> 777 Vanishing Lane
> Cardtrick, Nevada 89011
>
> Dear Catalog Department:
>
> I understand you sell books and props for magicians. Please send me your catalog so I can see what you have available.
>
> I am an amateur magician and would like to make money this summer performing at parties in my neighborhood.
>
> I will need to decide what to order in time to practice for my summer shows, so please send the catalog as soon as possible. Thank you for your help.
>
> Sincerely,
>
> *Grayson Parks*
> Parks the Magnificent

Good-Looking Action Letters

When you write a business or action letter, you want to be taken seriously. A good-looking letter is more likely to get attention.

Guidelines for Action Letters

- Use a margin of at least one inch (or 2 1/2 centimeters) on the sides, top, and bottom of the page. For short letters, use wider margins.
- Skip one to four lines between the heading (or letterhead) and the date.
- Leave four lines between the date and the inside address.
- Skip one line between the inside address and the salutation, and between the salutation and the body of the letter.
- You can indent the first line of each paragraph or keep the lines even. A paragraph you don't indent is called *flush-left* and is preferred for business letters.
- Skip one line between paragraphs.
- Leave one line between the body of your letter and the closing.
- Leave four lines to sign your name. Below your signature, print or type your name (and your title if you're using one).

Your Turn: Getting Action

When might you want to write a business or action letter?

List two reasons you might want to write a business letter. To whom would you write for each thing on your list? If you need help, ask friends or adults for ideas.

Two reasons I could write an action letter are . . .

1. _____

_____

2. _____

_____

To get action, I would write to . . .

1. _____

_____

2. _____

Making a Plan

When you write a business or action letter, make it clear exactly what you want. Start by making a plan. List what you need to say in your letter.

❶ **Why you are writing:** Begin by clearly stating the reason for your letter. Make sure your reader knows the topic from the start.

❷ **Why it's important:** Explain why the reader should care about your topic or concern. People pay more attention when they believe something is important.

> **MAILBOX REMINDER**
> **Plan . . . List**
> **Draft . . . Proofread**
> **Write . . . and Address**

❸ **What you want done:** Instead of just criticizing or complaining, share your ideas about what could be done. Think of how you would feel if someone said, "Do something!" but didn't offer any helpful suggestions.

Things to Think About

- People are busy. Keep your letter short.
- Start with the most important thing.
- When you tell why your concern is important, give examples or facts.
- Don't insult anyone. You can disagree, but be polite.
- Say something positive if you can.
- Always suggest a solution. What action do you want the person to take?
- Stick to one topic. If you want to tell the person about something else, write another letter.

Your Turn: Make a Plan

Make a plan for an action letter. Choose one of the ideas you wrote on page 43 or think of something new. Make a plan below.

❶ My problem, request, or concern _____

_____

_____

❷ Why it is important (some examples) _____

_____

_____

_____

_____

❸ The action I want taken _____

_____

_____

The Better Letter Book
© The Learning Works, Inc.

Making a Complaint

When you receive poor service or buy something that isn't worth the money, how do you feel? Disappointed? Angry? Like there's nothing you can do? There is, in fact, something you can do. You can write a complaint letter.

A complaint letter should be short, courteous, and filled with facts. Plan your letter. Make a list of the main points.

The 1-2-3's of Making Complaints

❶ **Your complaint:** State the problem. Be clear and concise.

❷ **The facts:** Give details of the incident or situation. Include dates, times, places, costs, and a brief description.

❸ **The solution:** Suggest how the problem can be solved or what you would like the business or company to do. Be reasonable about what you expect.

Melissa Murray
64 Skyview Avenue
Celestial, Massachusetts 02022

July 14, 1995

Customer Service Department
Green Moon Telescope Company
321 Starway Blvd.
Orion, Pennsylvania 19311

Dear Customer Service Representative:

The telescope I ordered from your company arrived with a broken lens.

I ordered the refracting telescope, Model S-12, in early May. When it arrived on July 10, the box was crushed, and the lens was cracked.

I want to return this telescope and get a replacement or my money back. I don't think I should have to pay the return postage. Please tell me how to return it at your expense.

Sincerely,

Melissa Murray

Melissa Murray

MAILBOX TIP
If you don't receive an answer to your complaint, try sending a copy of your letter to the Better Business Bureau in your town or to the local newspaper's consumer complaint column.

❶ **Your complaint**

❷ **The facts**

❸ **The solution**

Your Turn: Make a Complaint

Choose one of these problems and write a complaint letter.

- You bought a video game made by Visionizer, a company at 100 Information Highway, Multimedia, Arizona, 85022. The game has poor graphics, and you don't like playing it.

- For years, your soccer team has held its awards ceremony at Donny's Pizza. This year, when your coach calls, someone at the restaurant refuses to take a reservation for a group of kids. Donny's is located at 47 Pepperoni Place, Mozzarella, Florida, 33670.

- You were at the local jewelry store to buy your sister a birthday gift. The clerk ignored you and served all the adults, even though you were there first. Write to the owner, Mr. Garnet, at Gems and Stones, 65 Facet Street, Diamond, Iowa, 50082.

MAILBOX TIP
Here's how to address your letter:
- **For a company, write to the customer service representative.**
- **For a store, write to the owner.**
- **For a restaurant, write to the manager.**

Writing to Praise

Has anyone in a store or restaurant been especially nice to you or gone out of the way to be helpful? You can be nice in return by writing a complimentary letter to the person's supervisor or to the company president. Send a copy to the person who was nice to you, too. Complimentary letters are important because they say that someone is doing a good job and deserves recognition.

The 1-2-3's of Complimentary Letters

❶ **Introduction:** Name or describe the person.

❷ **Action:** Describe what the person did and tell when and where it happened.

❸ **Compliment:** Tell how you feel about the person or what he or she did.

> **MAILBOX TIP**
>
> To write a complimentary letter to someone in your city or town, look up the address in your phone book.

Piper Beatty
123 Research Way
Discovery, Georgia 30332

February 8, 1997

Dr. Reed Bookman
County Library Director
987 Library Lane
Discovery, Georgia 30332

Dear Mr. Bookman:

Last Saturday, the research librarian at the Reading Street Library helped me a lot. I don't know his name, but he wears glasses, has red hair, and was there from 3:30 to closing.

I had to do a science report on Stephen Hawking, but most of the good books were checked out. The librarian showed me how to do an on-line computer search. Then he taught me to use the microfiche machine.

I really appreciate all the help the librarian gave me. I think you should know what a great librarian he is.

Sincerely yours,

Piper Beatty

Piper Beatty

❶ **Introduction**

❷ **Action**

❸ **Compliment**

Your Turn: Give a Compliment

Think of someone who went out of his or her way to help you recently. Write a complimentary letter to the person's boss or company and tell what the person did that was special.

Here are some ideas:

- a fast-food worker
- a great teacher
- a clerk in a store
- a custodian

MAILBOX REMINDER

Plan ... List
Draft ... Proofread ... Write
Remember to write by the numbers, 1-2-3.

Requesting Information

When you write reports, essays, and papers, you can find most of the information you need in your school or local library. But sometimes you need something more specific or up-to-date. You can get information by requesting it in a letter.

The 1-2-3's of Requests

❶ **Identification:** Tell a little about yourself and why you need information.

❷ **Explanation:** Ask for only what you need and tell how you plan to use it. Describe your assignment or explain why you are interested in the topic.

❸ **Thank you:** Maps and pamphlets are expensive. Companies, organizations, and public agencies do you a favor by sending material, so be sure to say thank you.

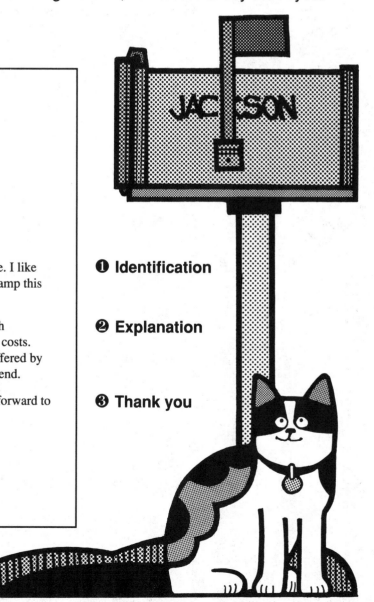

Susan Jackson
Route 3, Box 2
Kilobyte, Oregon 97301

January 12, 1996

Camp Tech
P. O. Box 65911
Online, Ohio 43002

Dear Camp Staff Member:

I am eleven years old, and I am in the fifth grade. I like computers and would like to go to a computer camp this summer.

Please send me a brochure about your camp with information on your program, the dates, and the costs. I want to compare the costs and the programs offered by different camps before I decide which one to attend.

Thank you for your time and help. I'm looking forward to learning about your camp.

Sincerely,

Susan Jackson
Susan Jackson

❶ Identification

❷ Explanation

❸ Thank you

Your Turn: Make a Request

Write a letter to the chamber of commerce for one of the states listed below. Ask for information about natural resources, population, and major industries for a report you are doing at school. How will you find the correct address for the chamber of commerce you choose?

Alaska	New Mexico	Mississippi
Utah	Illinois	Pennsylvania

Expressing an Idea or Opinion

The wonderful thing about the country where you live is that you are free to have an opinion and express it. Your opinion is important. If you feel strongly about saving forests, getting a swimming pool at your local park, or having more lunch choices at your school, write to the people in charge.

The 1-2-3's of Sharing Opinions

❶ **What you think:** Decide what you want the reader to know and state your opinion clearly.

❷ **Why you think that:** Give at least two reasons for your opinion.

❸ **What you suggest:** Suggest a change or describe what you wish were true.

Where to Send Opinions

The Media

- Newspapers or magazines
- TV or radio stations
- Your school newsletter

The People in Charge

- Public officials
- Heads of organizations

Carly Martino
237 Newthot Avenue
Faircity, Pennsylvania 19040

February 8, 1995

Editor-in-Chief
Faircity Daily Times
783 Newsprint Avenue
Faircity, Pennsylvania 19040

Dear Editor:

I think newspapers need to report the good things kids do. All the news about kids seems to be bad.

Last Sunday, I found six stories about kids in your paper. Every story was about someone in trouble. I know lots of kids who make good grades, help in the community, and do what's right.

I wish you would ask your reporters to get news about the good things kids do. Those kids deserve to be noticed.

Sincerely,

Carly Martino

Carly Martino

Your Turn: Improve This Letter

Imagine your friend wrote an angry letter to the principal. Write a new letter that states your friend's opinion in a better way. Remember the numbers, 1-2-3.

October 3, 1997

Principal Evans:

I think your idea of closing the computer room during lunch is stupid.

Lots of us do math and stuff on the computers at lunch. If we can't get in the computer room, we'll get bored and you might be sorry.

If you close the computer room at lunch, kids will hate this school.

A warning from a computer room user

MAILBOX TIP
When you write an opinion letter, think about the person who will read it.
Angry letters make readers feel angry, too.

The Better Letter Book
© The Learning Works, Inc.

Writing for a Cause

Your neighborhood park is full of trash. Floods are driving farmers in your state from their homes. Companies are pouring chemicals into the nearby river. What can you do?

Write a letter. Tell company presidents or public officials how you feel about a problem. Ask them to help find a solution. If you can, say something positive about the person to whom you're writing or about the situation.

The 1-2-3's of Writing for a Cause

❶ **Concern:** Make the problem clear.

❷ **Importance:** Give facts or examples that show why it's important.

❸ **Suggestion:** Offer a solution.

Jonathan Day
161 Caution Court
Santa Terra, Texas 78750

March 22, 1995

Superintendent of Schools
Santa Terra District Office
1 Learning Street
Santa Terra, Texas 78750

Dear Superintendent:

I'm in the fifth grade at Booker School. A corner near the school is dangerous. Cars speed through the crosswalk on Lake without slowing down.

Last week, when my friend Kyle crossed the street, he was almost hit by a car. The kids in my school are afraid somebody will get hurt.

My dad says you want schools to be safe. I knew you'd want to know about this problem.

Will you please hire a crossing guard for the corner of Lake and West Union Avenue?

Sincerely yours,

Jonathan Day

Jonathan Day

❶ **Concern**

❷ **Importance**

Something positive (optional)

❸ **Suggestion**

Your Turn: What Is Your Cause?

Choose a cause from the list below or think of your own.

- to support or oppose gun control
- to suggest $1 movies for kids on Saturdays
- to get bike lanes on city streets
- to get more library books on sports

After you pick a cause, make a plan below. Decide exactly what you want to ask for. Plan a letter you can write. Include something positive if you can.

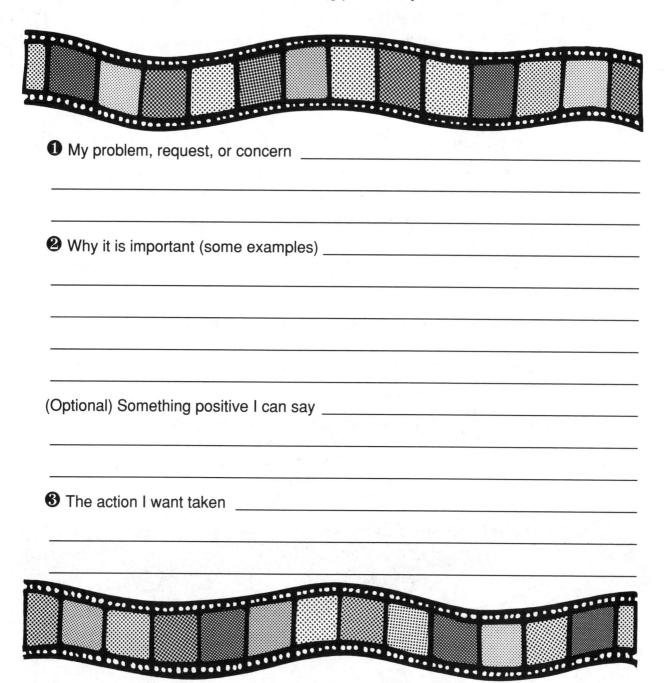

❶ My problem, request, or concern _____

_____

_____

❷ Why it is important (some examples) _____

_____

_____

_____

(Optional) Something positive I can say _____

_____

_____

❸ The action I want taken _____

_____

_____

Writing to Public Officials

Promoting a Cause to Public Officials

Sometimes public officials pay special attention to kids, especially if the cause is an important one. When you write to an elected official, you often get a letter back. So grab your pen and make yourself heard!

Tips for Writing to Public or Government Officials

- Write a legislator one month before the legislative session begins so he or she has time to read and think about your letter.
- Use the official's name and title. If you don't know or aren't sure, check your phone book or call your local library.
- Be specific. Use examples that show your letter is sincere and thoughtfully written.

To Whom Would You Write?

For each of these problems, decide which official you could write to for help. Could you write to more than one official about the same problem? Look on page 57 for ideas.

Your town library needs more money to buy books.

_____

_____

You want to increase the size and number of state or provincial parks.

_____

_____

You want your country to stop buying products from countries that kill whales.

_____

_____

Where to Write

Here's how to address, begin, and end letters to U.S. and Canadian public officials. To find addresses for local and other officials, check your phone book or public library.

President of the United States: Write to the president about things that affect the entire country or the United States and other nations.

> The President
> The White House
> Washington, DC 20500
> Dear Mr. President:
> Respectfully yours,

U.S. Senator: Write to your senator about issues or laws that affect the nation or national issues that affect your state.

> The Honorable (senator's full name)
> United States Senate
> Washington, DC 20510
> Dear Senator (last name):
> Respectfully yours,

U.S. Representative: Write to your representative about issues or laws that affect the nation or national issues that affect your state or your community.

> The Honorable (representative's full name)
> House of Representatives
> Washington, DC 20515
> Dear Representative (last name):
> Respectfully yours,

State Legislator: Write to your state legislator about issues that affect your state or its services.

> The Honorable (legislator's full name)
> (state's name) State Capitol
> (city, state, and zip code)
> Dear (title and last name):
> Sincerely yours,

Governor: Write to your governor about issues that affect your state or its services.

> The Honorable (governor's full name)
> Governor of (state's name)
> (city, state, and zip code)
> Dear Governor (last name):
> Sincerely yours,

Mayor: Write to your mayor about issues that affect your city, town, or neighborhood.

> The Honorable (mayor's full name)
> Office of the Mayor
> (street address)
> (town, state, and zip code)
> Dear Mayor (last name):
> Sincerely yours,

Prime Minister of Canada: Write to the prime minister about things that involve the Parliament or Canada and other nations.

> The Right Honourable (prime minister's full name)
> Prime Minister of Canada
> Langeven Block
> 80 Wellington Street
> Ottawa, ON K1A 0A3
> Dear Mr. or Madame Prime Minister:
> Respectfully yours,

Governor General of Canada: Write to the governor general about issues of concern to the queen's representative.

> His or Her Excellency the Right Honourable (full name)
> Rideau Hall, 1 Sussex Drive
> Ottawa, ON K1A 0A1
> Dear Governor General:
> Respectfully yours,

Member of the House of Commons: Write to your member of the house about issues that affect your country, province, or territory.

> The Honourable (member's full name)
> House of Commons
> 111 Wellington Street
> Ottawa, ON K1A 0A6
> Dear Mr. or Madame (last name):
> Respectfully yours,

Member of the Senate: Write to your senator about issues that affect your country, province, or territory.

> The Honourable (senator's full name)
> The Parliament Building
> 111 Wellington Street
> Ottawa, ON K1A 0A6
> Dear Senator (last name):
> Respectfully yours,

Premier of a Province: Write to your premier about issues or laws that affect your province.

> The Honourable (premier's full name)
> Premier of the Province of (name)
> (town, province, and postal code)
> Dear Mr. or Madame Premier:
> Respectfully yours,

Mayor: Write to your mayor about things that involve your city, town, or neighbourhood.

> His or Her Worship Mayor (mayor's full name)
> City Hall
> (street address)
> (town, province, and postal code)
> Dear Mr. or Madame Mayor:
> Respectfully yours,

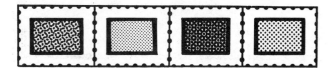

57

Your Turn: Write for a Cause

Choose a cause and write to someone who can help. You can use the work you did on pages 55 and 56, or you can choose a new cause.

MAILBOX REMINDER
Plan ... List
Draft ... Proofread ... Write
Remember to write by the numbers: 1, 2, 3.

About Addresses for Envelopes

Everyone knows that if a letter has the wrong address on the envelope, it won't get where it's supposed to go. But even with the correct address, letters can be delayed. Why?

Most postal workers in big-city post offices use machines to do their work. They watch thousands of letters move past like trains on a track. They have to read the addresses — *FAST!* Then they punch a key to send each letter down a new track to where it needs to go.

What do you think happens if the worker can't read someone's writing? The letter may go to the wrong place. It may be set aside until someone has time to figure out where it belongs. When a letter needs special treatment, it gets delayed — for days or even weeks. Sometimes it never arrives at all.

Printed Addresses

Addresses printed with a printer or a good typewriter can be read by computer-run machines. Using all capital letters helps the computer read your addresses more easily. Use the official postal abbreviations for states or provinces. Put everything on the correct line. If you don't, you'll confuse the machine.

If you can't address your envelope on a computer or typewriter, print neatly in ink. Use this order, but include only what you need.

- Person's name
- Office or department
- Company
- Apartment, suite, or floor
- Street address (or post office box)
- City, state or province, and postal or zip code

See page 2 for a list of state and province abbreviations.

> **MAILBOX TIP**
> You can put the apartment number, suite, or floor on the same line as the street address, but not on the line *after* the street address.

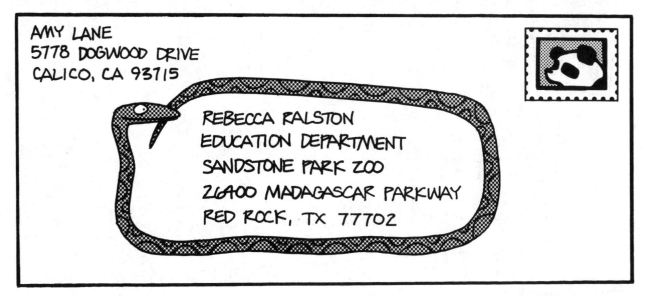

The Better Letter Book
© The Learning Works, Inc.

About Postcards

Writing letters is a wonderful way to share your news. But sometimes when you're on a vacation or traveling, there's no time to write a letter. Instead, send a postcard.

A postcard is made of heavy paper or card stock. It's usually 3 1/2" x 5 1/2 " (about 9 cm x 14 cm). Plain postcards you buy at the post office are already stamped. These and picture postcards are cheaper to send than letters.

Put the address of the person to whom you are sending your postcard in the space provided. Write your note in the space for the message. Be sure to write clearly.

> **SHHHHHH . . .**
> It's best not to write anything personal on a postcard. Everyone who handles the card has a chance to read it. Write a letter when what you have to say is private.

July 14

Dear Rachel Rae,
This zoo is so awesome!
There are all kinds of animals I've never seen before – like angwantibos and douroucoulis (yes, those are really animals!). I got to scratch a giant tortoise under her chin and rub the face of a huge, wet, _very_ sweet walrus.
I'll have LOTS to tell you when I get home on Tuesday.!!
Love, Tracy

Megan Mezori
240 W. Romano
Bluebell. KY 42010

Rachel Rae Benton
926 Paddock Place
Bluebell, KY 42010

Make Your Own Postcards

You can make your own postcards by using a sheet of card stock and decorating it with drawings, stickers, or photographs.

You will need

- 1 sheet of 8 1/2" x 11" card stock
- stickers, stamps, drawing pens, or a photograph or cartoon
- ruler
- scissors
- pencil

Directions

Lay the card stock lengthwise. Using your ruler, divide it into four sections (3 1/2" x 5 1/2" inches or 9 cm x 14 cm). Cut with your scissors.

You can design your postcard in two ways. If you have a short message, divide one side of the card in half; use one-half for your message and one-half for the address. Decorate the other side of the card. Try these ideas, or use your own:

- Draw a picture.
- Paste a photograph.
- Use stickers or stamps.
- Paste a comic strip or cartoon.

Or, you can use one side of your card for the message and one side for the address. Decorate your card with a border or a small picture so you have a clear space in which to write.

MAILBOX TIP
When you decorate your card, make sure the postal carrier will be able to read the address easily.

About Stationery

Stationery can be simple white paper, it can be lined, or it can be colorful. Most decorative writing papers come in sets with paper and envelopes that match.

Writing paper comes in many sizes. Sometimes the paper and envelopes are sold separately. Make sure you choose envelopes that are the right size for the paper you buy.

Letterhead stationery can have your name and address or just your name or initials printed on the paper. To make your own letterhead, type your name and address at the top of your stationery. Your letterhead can be centered at the top of the page, or it can be in the top-left or top-right corner.

You can use a computer to design a letterhead. Then you can print your letterhead stationery when you need it. You can also print one page with your letterhead and take it to a copy center to make copies on different colors or types of paper.

Jill Merryweather 10 Showers Road Sunnytown, Florida 33333	**Jill Merryweather** 10 Showers Road • Sunnytown, Florida 33333	Jill Merryweather 10 Showers Road Sunnytown, Florida 33333

Make Your Own Stationery

You can turn plain white paper into your own personal stationery by using your imagination.

Directions

Plain white paper is best for this project. Do not use notebook paper or yellow tablet paper. Choose envelopes that fit the paper.

You will need:

- poster paints
- a household sponge
- foil pie plates or shallow pans
- white paper towels
- scrap paper
- white writing paper you have chosen

1. Cut the sponge into small shapes such as circles, hearts, squares, or triangles.

2. Use a separate container for each color of paint. Pour a small amount of paint into each pie plate or pan.

3. Dip the sponge into the paint and then blot off any extra paint on a paper towel.

4. Press the paint-covered surface of the sponge onto some scrap paper for practice. Lift the sponge straight up so you do not smear the print. Practice until your prints are clear.

5. Apply this method to one section of your writing paper. Try making a border, decorating the corners, or putting designs across the top or bottom of the paper. Because you can't write over poster paint, you need to limit where you put your designs.

6. Let each sheet dry before you use it for stationery.

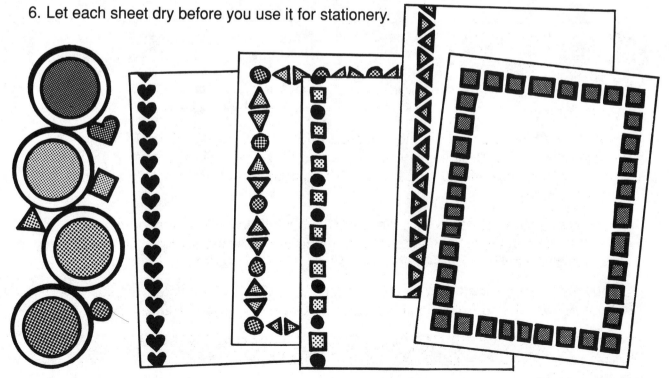

The Better Letter Book
© The Learning Works, Inc.

Codes and Stamps

Postal and Zip Codes

Each country decides its own postal codes, so codes are different from one country to the next. In the United States, they are called zip codes. In Canada, they are called postal codes. You need a code on every letter you mail. Without one, your letter will take longer to get where it's going. It might not get there at all.

If you don't know the zip or postal code for the address of the person you are writing to, you can call or visit your local post office. Most post offices have a directory you can use to look up a code. If you have trouble using the directory, ask someone for help.

Postage

Most letters you write will get where they're going if they have a standard first-class postage stamp. Sometimes, however, you will need more postage. Sometimes you can use even less.

Here are some factors that determine how much postage you need:

- weight
- size (length, width, and thickness)
- type of item (letter, postcard, or package)
- destination (within or outside the country)
- special handling (certified mail, priority mail, etc.)

If you need to find out current postal rates, call or visit your post office. Most post offices will give you an information sheet that lists the current rates.

> ### MAILBOX FACT
> **In a single year, the U.S. Postal Service issues almost 27 million stamps, enough to stretch around the earth 17 times.**

Fun with Stamps

Stamp collecting is one of the most popular hobbies in the world. The U.S Postal Service sponsors 35,000 Benjamin Franklin Stamp Clubs in public and private elementary schools. The clubs are named for Benjamin Franklin because he was the first U.S. Postmaster General.

If you want to start a stamp-collecting club at your school, ask a teacher or your principal to talk to your local postmaster or to write to the Ben Franklin Stamp Club Coordinator, U.S. Postal Service, P.O. Box 449994, Kansas City, MO 64144-9994.

If you're interested in starting your own stamp collection, write a letter requesting a free booklet from Stamp Collecting Made Easy, P.O. Box 29, Sydney, OH 45365.